THE LORD'S PRAYER
A COURSE FOR THE CHRISTIAN JOURNEY

Church Publishing
NEW YORK

Authors and Contributor

Authors

Stephen Cottrell is the Bishop of Chelmsford
Steven Croft is the Bishop of Sheffield
Paula Gooder is a leading New Testament writer and lecturer
Robert Atwell is the Bishop of Stockport
Sharon Ely Pearson is a Christian educator in The Episcopal Church

Contributor

Loretta Minghella is the Director of Christian Aid

pilgrim

THE LORD'S PRAYER
A COURSE FOR THE CHRISTIAN JOURNEY

STEPHEN COTTRELL
STEVEN CROFT
PAULA GOODER
ROBERT ATWELL
SHARON ELY PEARSON

Contribution from
LORETTA MINGHELLA

Church Publishing
NEW YORK

First published in the United Kingdom in 2013 by

Church House Publishing
Church House
Great Smith Street
London SW1P 3AZ

First published in the United States in 2016 by

Church Publishing, Incorporated.
19 East 34th Street
New York, New York 10016
www.churchpublishing.org

Cover and contents design by David McNeill, Revo Design.

Library of Congress Cataloging-in-Publication Data

A record of this book is available from the Library of Congress.

ISBN-13: 978-0-89869-940-1 (pbk.)
ISBN-13: 978-0-89869-941-8 (ebook)

Printed in the United States of America

CONTENTS

WELCOME TO *PILGRIM*

Welcome to this course of exploration into the truth of the Christian faith as it has been revealed in Jesus Christ and lived out in his Church down through the centuries.

The aim of this course is to help people explore what it means to become disciples of Jesus Christ. From the very beginning of his ministry, Jesus called people to follow him and become his disciples. The Church in every generation shares in the task of helping others hear Christ's call to them and follow him.

We hope the course will help you to understand this faith and to see how it can be lived out each day, and that it will equip you to make a decision about whether to be part of this Church. This will either happen by being baptized and confirmed, if this has not happened to you before, or by a renewal of baptismal vows.

You won't be able to find out everything about the Christian faith in any one course. But through the *Pilgrim* course material you will be able to reflect on some of the great texts that have been particularly significant to Christian people from the earliest days of the Church:

- The Creeds
- The Lord's Prayer
- The Beatitudes
- The Commandments

There is one book based on each of these texts in the "Follow" stage of *Pilgrim* (designed for absolute beginners) and one that goes further in the "Grow" (discipleship) stage.

By learning these texts, reflecting upon them, and seeing what they mean for your life, you will make a journey through the great story of the Christian faith. And you will do this in the company of a small group of fellow travelers: people like you who want to find out more about the Christian faith and are considering its claims and challenges.

In other words, this course is for people who are *not yet Christians*, but who are open to finding out more and *for those who are just beginning the journey*. People who want some sort of *refresher course* are also very welcome. In walking with you on this journey we are not assuming that you necessarily share the beliefs that are being explored, just that you want to find out about them.

This course will approach the great issues of faith not by trying to persuade you to believe, but by encouraging you to practice the ancient disciplines of biblical reflection and prayer which have always been at the heart of the living out of Christian faith.

We don't think these are things that should only be practiced once you have come to faith. Rather, they can be the means by which faith is received and then strengthened within us.

Each book has six or seven sessions, and in each session you will find:

- a **theme**
- some **opening prayers**
- a **"conversation-starter"**
- an opportunity to **reflect** on a **reading** from Scripture (the Bible)
- a short **article** from a contemporary Christian writer on the theme
- some **questions** to address
- a further time of **prayer**
- finally, a **"sending out"** section, with suggestions for further reflection and selected quotations from the great tradition of Christian writing to help you do so.

This pattern of contemplation and discussion will, we believe, help you to decide whether you wish to respond to Christ and be part of his Church. Remember that the Church is not a group of men and women who are, themselves, certain about all these things, but who "believe, with God's help" (this is what you are asked at baptism) and then go on following Jesus Christ and continuing the journey of faith.

We all learn in different ways, and there is a variety of material here to support you. Different people will receive something from the different parts of the session according to their own learning style.

At the end of this course, we hope you will have made some new friends and explored quite a lot of areas of Christian faith. Just as importantly, you will have been given confidence to read the Bible prayerfully and critically, and you will have, if you wish, established a pattern for prayer. We hope that *Pilgrim* will help you lay a foundation for a lifetime of learning more about God's love revealed in Jesus Christ and what it means to be his disciple.

This little book gives you all you need to begin this great journey. You are standing where millions of men and women have stood: you have caught a glimpse of who God is, and you are puzzled and curious to know whether the claims of the Christian faith can be trusted and whether they actually make any difference to life.

This book and this course can help you. You will need the book for each session, but outside of the sessions you may want to look each week at the material you are about to study together. As the course goes on, you may want to take time each week to look back at what you have already covered as you move forward on your own pilgrimage.

INTRODUCTION TO *THE LORD'S PRAYER*

Long ago, when Christians were first learning about the faith, people would prepare for baptism as adults over two or three years. The final part of their journey would be in the season of Lent, preparing for baptism at Easter.

During the final part of the journey, the bishop would teach them about some of the greatest treasures of the Christian faith. One of the most important was the prayer we know as the Lord's Prayer.

This prayer was only taught to and said by Christians. You couldn't look it up in a book (there were no printed books then). It was one of the special things you were given as you prepared for your baptism. You would learn it by heart and teach it to your household.

Reflect for a moment on the wonder of this special prayer, used by every generation of Christians there has ever been. For some, the words are very familiar. Perhaps we learned them as children, but perhaps we have never thought about what they mean for adults. For some, the words are too familiar—we have given up thinking about what they mean. But for some, the words will be new, something precious to be explored on the way to becoming a disciple of Jesus Christ.

One of the early Church Fathers said that the whole of the Christian gospel—the whole of the good news—is in the Lord's Prayer if we truly understand it.

We are going to explore the Lord's Prayer in these sessions as a gateway to the Christian gospel, as a guide to our own prayers, and as a way of deepening our relationship with God.

This prayer is used all around the world by millions of people worldwide and has been for 2,000 years. There probably isn't a moment, day or night, when there isn't someone on earth praying the Lord's Prayer.

There probably isn't a language on earth that doesn't contain a version of the Lord's Prayer.

You can pray this prayer when you are full of joy. You can pray it in the ordinary days. It's used at services of baptism and weddings as we celebrate great family events. It's used at the bedside of someone who is dying and at their funeral service.

The Lord's Prayer is found in a slightly different form in two of the four Gospels (the accounts of Jesus' life and teaching) we find in the Bible: the Gospel of Matthew and the Gospel of Luke. In both Gospels, the words of the prayer are given by Jesus. The setting for the prayer gives us an idea of why Jesus gives us this prayer as a precious resource for our faith.

Luke puts the Lord's Prayer in Chapter 11 of his Gospel in the context of Jesus' own prayers. The disciples see the difference that prayer makes to the Lord. But they also know that they struggle with their own prayers. They don't know what to say or do. So the disciples ask Jesus a key question as he returns from his prayers one morning: *Lord, teach us to pray.*

Think about this request for a moment. It's a request that implies that prayer is a very important activity. But it's a request which implies that prayer is something we need to learn to do.

Jesus replies by giving them a prayer to pray. It is a very brief prayer and one that anyone can memorize from an early age. Yet each line in the prayer is rich and powerful. This is the prayer that teaches us to pray.

Matthew sets the prayer in the center of the collection of Jesus' teachings and sayings known as the Sermon on the Mount. Again, it follows some basic teaching on how to pray. Prayer is not about showing off and standing on street corners but about developing a secret, inner relationship with God. It's not about the ability to string words together and impress other people but about simplicity and sincerity.

Then Jesus offers these words for prayer which give us a way of keeping to his teachings. The Lord's Prayer is brief compared to other prayers of the day. The Lord's Prayer is something anyone can learn by heart and so use in private, in that hidden room, as we come to our prayers: *Pray then in this way*.

God is approachable. Prayer is something anyone can do. You don't have to use complicated words or flowery language. God isn't swayed by arguments or by length or by skill in prayer.

Here are some words you can say, but here also is a deep pattern for prayer.

Here is a way of seeing God, the world, and yourself that is profound, revolutionary, and good news.

The Lord's Prayer

Our Father in heaven,
hallowed be your name,
your kingdom come,
your will be done,
on earth as in heaven.
Give us today our daily bread.
Forgive us our sins
as we forgive those who sin against us.
Save us from the time of trial,
and deliver us from evil.
For the kingdom, the power,
and the glory are yours
now and for ever.
Amen.

CONTEMPORARY LANGUAGE VERSION

Our Father, who art in heaven,
hallowed be thy name;
thy kingdom come;
thy will be done;
on earth as it is in heaven.
Give us this day our daily bread.
And forgive us our trespasses,
as we forgive those who trespass against us.
And lead us not into temptation;
but deliver us from evil.
For thine is the kingdom,
and the power, and the glory,
for ever and ever.
Amen.

TRADITIONAL LANGUAGE VERSION

SESSION ONE:
OUR FATHER IN HEAVEN,
HALLOWED BE YOUR NAME

pilgrim

The aim of this session is to explore and experience the truth that Jesus invites us into a new relationship with God as our Father in prayer and we are sisters and brothers together.

Opening Prayers

O God, make speed to save us.
O Lᴏʀᴅ, make haste to help us.

As a father cares for his children,
so does the Lᴏʀᴅ care for those who fear him.

PSALM 103:13

O Lᴏʀᴅ, I am not proud;
I have no haughty looks.

I do not occupy myself with great matters,
or with things that are too hard for me.

But I still my soul and make it quiet,
   like a child upon its mother's breast;
my soul is quieted within me.

O Israel, wait upon the Lᴏʀᴅ,
from this time forth for evermore.

PSALM 131:1-4

But whenever you pray, go into your room and shut the door and pray
to your Father who is in secret; and your Father who sees in secret will
reward you.

MATTHEW 6:6

Loving Father,
strengthen our hearts by your Holy Spirit.
Grant us power with all the saints
to appreciate how wide and long and high and deep
is the love of Christ.
Amen.

BASED ON EPHESIANS 3:16-19

Conversation

What is your earliest memory of saying the Lord's Prayer? How old were you? Who taught you to say the words?

Reflecting on Scripture

Reading

According to the gospels, Jesus himself gives the prayer to his disciples. We find the prayer in two different places. In Luke 11:1-4, Jesus gives the prayer when the disciples say to him: "Lord, teach us to pray." In Matthew's gospel, Jesus teaches his disciples to pray in the central section of the Sermon on the Mount.

"And whenever you pray, do not be like the hypocrites; for they love to stand and pray in the synagogues and at the street corners, so that they may be seen by others. Truly I tell you, they have received their reward. [6]But whenever you pray, go into your room and shut the door and pray to your Father who is in secret; and your Father who sees in secret will reward you.
[7]"When you are praying, do not heap up empty phrases as the Gentiles do; for they think that they will be heard because of their many words. [8]Do not be like them, for your Father knows what you need before you ask him.
[9]"Pray then in this way: Our Father in heaven, hallowed be your name. [10]Your kingdom come. Your will be done, on earth as it is in heaven. [11]Give us this day our daily bread. [12]And forgive us our debts, as we also have forgiven our debtors. [13]And do not bring us to the time of trial, but rescue us from the evil one. [14]For if you forgive others their trespasses, your heavenly Father will also forgive you; [15]but if you do not forgive others, neither will your Father forgive your trespasses.

MATTHEW 6:5-15

- Read the passage through once.
- Keep a few moments' silence.
- Read the passage a second time with different voices.
- Invite everyone to say aloud a word or phrase that strikes them.
- Read the passage a third time.
- Share together what this word or phrase might mean and what questions it raises.

Reflection   STEVEN CROFT

Finding our place in the Universe

The first line of the Lord's Prayer summons you to discover your place in the universe. The prayer begins with the essential kindness of God and captures a sense of the Christian family. In just eight words the prayer leads us into the cosmic struggle which is taking place on the earth.

How does this one line help me find my place in the universe?

Through the very first word, "Father," Jesus invites us to call the Lord God, the creator of heaven and earth, Father. Jesus invites us into the same relationship with God which he himself enjoys.

Where do we fit into the created order?

We need to remember that in much of the Jewish tradition and in other religions, God is seen as all powerful and mighty. In Judaism, God is seen to be so holy that his name could not even be said out loud. But

Jesus encourages his disciples to address God simply, in a familiar way, as part of his family, as Father. In doing that we find our place in the universe.

Where do we fit into the created order? Did this beautiful world come about by chance? Our place in the universe is as children of our Father in heaven. We are not atoms floating in a sea of chaos or chance. The universe is not about randomness but relationship. We are created in God's image and likeness. We are made to know God and enjoy God for ever. To say "Our Father in heaven" is to stand by faith in the whole of that world view.

Humanity has turned away from God our creator and we have not lived in relationship with God. But God has sent us his Son. Jesus comes to us so that we can call God "Father." Through the life and ministry, death and resurrection of Jesus we can know God as Father. The words of the prayer are only possible because of the one who gives us the prayer.

What difference does the "Our" make in "Our Father"? Again, it is about finding our place in the universe. Every time we say this prayer, we remember that we are connected not only vertically to God but horizontally to others.

If you pray this prayer, you are part of a family. Does Jesus mean us to pray as though we are part of one big family of the entire human race? Or does he mean us to pray as though we are part of his own family— the Christian Church—the family of the disciples.

It's the second of these more than the first. The Lord's Prayer is taught to the disciples not the crowds. This is the Christian family prayer. We are brothers and sisters together and we have brothers and sisters around the world, our fellow Christians. This creates a tremendous sense of solidarity. It also creates a tremendous sense of responsibility for one another.

> **In short**
>
> In the Lord's Prayer we are invited to call God our Father. This gives us a sense of place in the universe and relationship with God and with each other.

For discussion

- How often do you use the Lord's Prayer? What version do you use?
- Can you see a pattern or shape in the prayer for our own prayers? What is the best way for you to pray?
- Does it raise any questions for you to address God as Father and to think of Christian people as your brothers and sisters?

Intimate—but not cozy

"In heaven" balances the intimacy of the word "Father" and reminds us who our Father is. There is, in Christian prayer, a balance between intimacy and reverence—between God with us and God the creator of the universe—far above us and beyond our comprehension. We hold both in our prayers. Our picture of God needs to be intimate but not cozy. It is possible to be too casual in our prayers and in our approach to God. We need reminding that God has larger concerns than our day-to-day anxieties, like whether we can find a parking space or not.

Finally, the first petition: "Hallowed be your name." The idea of God's name is a big idea in the Bible. God's name carries the idea of God's nature, identity, and love. The word "hallowed" means to make holy, to revere. So we are praying that God's very nature will be honored in every possible way in every part of the earth and for all time. We are praying that God's will be known and worshipped; that God's nature might be reflected in human society in justice, peace, and love, in joy, hope, healing, and tenderness.

The prayer takes us into the heart of the struggle of the universe. God's name and nature are *not* hallowed throughout the earth. In this prayer we place ourselves in that cosmic struggle. We place ourselves on God's side, for God, God's ways and God's nature. We offer ourselves in God's service and pledge ourselves to God's cause.

In short

"Hallowed be your name" reminds us of the awe and majesty of God. God is our Father in heaven, and his name—that which expresses his very nature—is something we reverence. By doing this we place ourselves firmly on God's side.

For discussion

- What does it mean for you to pray for God's name to be hallowed?

- How is the first line of the prayer good news for you, for those you love, and for the world?

Concluding Prayers

As our Savior taught us, so we pray: **Our Father**... (see p. 12)

We praise you, O God,
we acclaim you as the Lord;
all creation worships you,
the Father everlasting.
To you all angels, all the powers of heaven,
the cherubim and seraphim, sing in endless praise:
Holy, holy, holy Lord, God of power and might,
heaven and earth are full of your glory.

FROM TE DEUM LAUDAMUS

Let us bless the Lord:
Thanks be to God.

Sending Out

During this coming week, reflect on the first eight words of the Lord's Prayer and what they mean.

Reflect as well on the different ways in which you have prayed throughout your life. What will it mean to grow and deepen your relationship with God?

These readings may help you in your reflections:

> Just as the skill of a doctor is revealed in the care of his patients, so the nature of God is revealed through the way he relates to us.
>
> IRENAEUS (*C.* 130–*C.*200)

> Those who have been born again and restored to God through grace say "Father" at the beginning of all prayer because they are already beginning to be his sons and daughters... None of us would presume to do this had not Christ himself taught us to pray in this way. And if we are to call God "Father," then we ought to behave like sons and daughters of God, so that just as we are delighted to have God as our Father, so equally he can take delight in us his children.
>
> CYPRIAN OF CARTHAGE (*C.* 200–58)

> Late have I loved you, O beauty so ancient and so new; late have I loved you! For you were within me and I was in the external world and sought you there, and in my unlovely state I plunged into those lovely created things which you made. You were with me, and I was not with you. The lovely things kept me from you, though if they did not have their existence in you, they would have had no existence at all. You called and cried out loud to me and shattered my deafness. You were radiant and resplendent, you put to flight my blindness. You were fragrant, and I drew in my breath and now I pant after you. I tasted you and now I feel nothing but hunger and thirst for you. You touched me, and now I burn for your peace.
>
> AUGUSTINE (354–430)

YOUR KINGDOM COME, YOUR WILL BE DONE, ON EARTH AS IN HEAVEN

pilgrim

The aim of this session is to unpack the idea that the kingdom of God is central to Scripture, to Jesus' teaching, to the Lord's Prayer, and therefore to the Christian disciple.

Opening Prayers

O worship the L ORD in the beauty of holiness;
let the whole earth tremble before him.

PSALM 96:9

The earth is the L ORD 's and all that is in it,
the world and all who dwell therein.

For it is he who founded it upon the seas
and made it firm upon the rivers of the deep.

"Who shall ascend the hill of the L ORD
and who can stand in his holy place?"

"Those who have clean hands and a pure heart,
who have not pledged themselves to falsehood,
nor sworn by what is fraud.

They shall receive a blessing from the L ORD,
and a just reward from the God of their salvation."

Such is the generation of those who seek him,
of those who seek your face, O God of Jacob.

PSALM 24:1-6

Now after John was arrested, Jesus came to Galilee, proclaiming the good news of God, and saying, "The time is fulfilled, and the kingdom of God has come near; repent, and believe the good news."

MARK 1:14-15

O Trinity of love,
forgive us that we may forgive one another
heal us that we may be a people of healing
and renew us that we also may be makers of peace.
Amen.

THE IONA COMMUNITY WORSHIP BOOK (ADAPTED)

Conversation

If you could put just one thing right in the world, what would it be?

Reflecting on Scripture

Reading

The Book of Psalms is a collection of 150 songs and prayers. Psalm 99 is a hymn of praise which celebrates the truth that God is King and reigns over creation. God reigns eternally and Jesus came proclaiming the coming of his kingdom on earth.

The LORD is king; let the peoples tremble! He sits enthroned upon the cherubim; let the earth quake! ²The LORD is great in Zion; he is exalted over all the peoples. ³Let them praise your great and awesome name. Holy is he! ⁴Mighty King, lover of justice, you have established equity; you have executed justice and righteousness in Jacob. ⁵Extol the LORD our God; worship at his footstool. Holy is he! ⁶Moses and Aaron were among his priests, Samuel also was among those who called on his name. They cried to the LORD, and he answered them. ⁷He spoke to them in the pillar of cloud; they kept his decrees, and the statutes that he gave them. ⁸O LORD our God, you answered them; you were a forgiving God to them, but an avenger of their wrongdoings. ⁹Extol the LORD our God, and worship at his holy mountain; for the LORD our God is holy.

PSALM 99:1-9

Explanatory note

The *cherubim* in the Old Testament are angels whose wings hold up God's throne in heaven.

Zion refers to a mountain near Jerusalem, though it is often used, as here, as another term for Jerusalem, where the temple stood.

Jacob is another name for the nation of Israel.

Moses, Aaron, and *Samuel* are great figures from Israel's past. The story of the pillar of cloud is told in the book of Exodus, where it leads God's people through the Wilderness after their escape from Egypt.

- Read the passage through once.
- Keep a few moments' silence.
- Read the passage a second time with different voices.
- Invite everyone to say aloud a word or phrase that strikes them.
- Read the passage a third time.
- Share together what this word or phrase might mean and what questions it raises.

Reflection
LORETTA MINGHELLA

"The Lord is King"

The opening verses of Psalm 99 place faith firmly in the context of everyday life, claiming that God rules over the earth, both over the people of Zion and over all peoples. The Christian faith cannot, therefore, be relegated to the margins of society, or to some esoteric community. For the Lord's Prayer invites us to pray "your kingdom come" to acknowledge that God's reign over the universe is a reality but not yet fulfilled.

For a Christian to describe the Lord as king is to acknowledge the Church is part of something much larger. We are a community belonging to the kingdom of God. In the words of writer Brian McLaren, the Church is "a community that lives to see God's dream come true for the world." The Christian is a citizen and servant of the kingdom of God.

Life in the kingdom is one of personal and corporate responsibility; it is spiritual, and is highly practical. It focuses on who you are and how you live. Jesus came to announce that God's kingdom was near, but it is not yet here in all its fullness: it is something we long for and pray for and work for as Christian disciples. The question each of us must answer is "How can I live as a faithful member of God's kingdom?"

As well as describing God as "Mighty King," verse 4 declares that God is a "lover of justice"' who has "established equity." This powerful phrase tells us something of the character of God. To love someone, or something, is to be totally committed to them, it is to afford them priority in your life. It implies a willingness to give everything for them. That God loves justice elevates just acts, and just living, as an essential commitment.

Worship and service

The psalm also encourages us to worship God (in vv. 3, 5, and 9). Worship is offered to the One who is worthy. Worship is expressed in many ways, but not least through one's personal life choices. The greatest act of worship is to do that which pleases God; to reflect the character of God through obedient, loving service.

The Christian life is lived in a rhythm of worship and service. That service includes a love of justice and equity, and a commitment to work for these to be manifest throughout life globally. We cannot divorce faith from politics, or the local from the international. Justice must be applied universally, to everyone and by everyone.

> **In short**
>
> The Old Testament often describes God as King. God's kingdom is the place (heaven) where God's ideals of justice are lived out perfectly. We worship God in the whole of our lives by loving justice as much as God does.

For discussion

- What would life on earth look like if everyone acknowledged God as King over all?

- In what ways might your life need to change in order to serve the kingdom of God?

"Your kingdom come, your will be done, on earth as it is in heaven"

This phrase expresses a desire to see God's will, values, and priorities as the foundation of all social relationships. It is a statement of worship and intent, that we have a part to play in its fulfillment. Essentially it reminds us of the contrast between God's ideals and principles and those of earthly kingdoms or political structures.

To pray this is to desire an end to all kingdoms where injustice, oppression, and inequality dominate. It expresses a longing for hope and new relationships among all peoples. Seen like this, the kingdom of God is not so much about heaven as it is about life on earth, with justice and equity describing how people are to be treated: with the values of heaven.

Justice applies beyond all boundaries. It is relevant at all times and in every place, otherwise it cannot be described as justice. If God loves justice then God's kingdom will be marked by justice. Teaching his disciples to pray like this, Jesus set a vision before them, and he calls disciples of all ages to make it a reality. It is part of his teaching; we are to be a people learning the way of God, promoting healing and reconciliation, and above all love.

The kingdom is like...

Jesus told many parables to teach the qualities of God's kingdom. In Matthew 13:33 Jesus described it as being like yeast, saying that when yeast is mixed with flour it leavens, permeates the whole. The values of the kingdom are to permeate all of life, and the life of a Christian will exemplify them.

If kingdom values are to permeate all of life they must be applied to all, including the most disadvantaged and marginalized in society, those who are disempowered through poverty. A disciple of Jesus must take this seriously, if we are to express the values of God's kingdom. It will include caring for those trapped in poverty and injustice at home and throughout the world.

> **In short**
>
> When we pray for God's kingdom to come, we are asking for our world and our lives to be marked by the justice that God loves so much. As Christians we long for God's kingdom to come but also do everything that we can to ensure that we live justly now.

For discussion

- John Dominic Crossan said, "Heaven is in great shape; it is the earth that is problematic." What would it mean for us to take this seriously in the context of Jesus' teaching?

- The richest 1% of the world's population controls 40% of the world's wealth, while the poorest 50% own just 1%. What should it mean for us to pray "Your kingdom come" in the light of this reality?

Concluding Prayers

As our Savior taught us, so we pray: **Our Father**... (see p. 12)

Lord, make us instruments of your peace,
Where there is hatred, let us sow love;
Where there is injury, pardon;
Where there is discord, union;
Where there is doubt, faith;
Where there is despair, hope;
Where there is darkness, light;
Where there is sadness, joy.
Grant that we may not so much seek to be consoled, as to console;
to be understood, as to understand;
to be loved, as to love.

For it is in giving that we receive;
It is in pardoning that we are pardoned;
and it is in dying that we are born to eternal life.
Amen.

ATTRIBUTED TO ST. FRANCIS

Sending Out

During this coming week reflect on what it means to pray the words: "Your kingdom come, your will be done on earth as it is in heaven."

What does it mean for the way you pray and for the way you live out your Christian faith? What does it mean for your call and vocation to follow Christ?

These readings may help you in your reflections:

> When we pray "Your will be done on earth as in heaven" we are not praying that God may accomplish what he wills, but that we may be able to do what God wills.
>
> CYPRIAN OF CARTHAGE (*C.* 200–258)

> The will of God presents itself to us at each instant like an immense ocean which the desire of our hearts can never empty, but we can receive something of that ocean as our hearts expand by faith, trust, and love.
>
> JEAN-PIERRE DE CAUSSADE (1675–1751)

> A Christian Society is not going to arrive until most of us really want it: and we are not going to want it until we become fully Christian. I may repeat, "Do as you would be done by"… but I cannot really carry it out til I love my neighbor as myself: and I cannot learn to love my neighbor as myself until I learn to love God: and I cannot learn to love God except by learning to obey him.
>
> C. S. LEWIS (1898–1963)

GIVE US THIS DAY OUR DAILY BREAD

pilgrim

The aim of this session is to explore the ways in which God feeds God's people, and to understand what it means to pray the words: Give us this day our daily bread.

Opening Prayers

O God, make speed to save us.
O Lord, make haste to help us.

All creation looks to you
to give them their food in due season.

PSALM 104:29

Some wandered in desert wastes;
they found no way to a city where they might dwell.

They were hungry and thirsty;
their spirits languished within them.

Then they cried to the Lord in their trouble,
and he delivered them from their distress.

He put their feet on the straight path
to go to a city where they might dwell.

Let them give thanks to the Lord for his mercy
and the wonders he does for his children.

For he satisfies the thirsty
and fills the hungry with good things.

PSALM 107:4-9

Therefore do not worry, saying, "What will we eat?" or "What will we drink?" or "What will we wear?" For it is the Gentiles who strive for all these things, and indeed your heavenly Father knows that you need all these things. But strive first for the kingdom of God and his righteousness, and all these things will be given to you as well.

MATTHEW 6:31-33

Lord Jesus Christ, we thank you for all the benefits that you have won for us, for all the pains and insults that you have born for us. Most merciful redeemer, friend and brother, may we know you more clearly, love you more dearly and follow you more nearly, day by day. **Amen.**

AFTER RICHARD OF CHICHESTER (1253)

Conversation

What three things do you feel most thankful for this day?

Reflecting on Scripture

Reading

In the evening quails came up and covered the camp; and in the morning there was a layer of dew around the camp. [14]When the layer of dew lifted, there on the surface of the wilderness was a fine flaky substance, as fine as frost on the ground. [15]When the Israelites saw it, they said to one another, "What is it?" For they did not know what it was. Moses said to them, "It is the bread that the LORD has given you to eat. [16]This is what the LORD has commanded: 'Gather as much of it as each of you needs, an omer to a person according to the number of persons, all providing for those in their own tents.'" [17]The Israelites did so, some gathering more, some less. [18]But when they measured it with an omer, those who gathered much had nothing over, and those who gathered little had no shortage; they gathered as much as each of them needed. [19]And Moses said to them, "Let no one leave any of it over until morning." [20]But they did not listen to Moses; some left part of it until morning, and it bred worms and became foul. And Moses was angry with them. [21]Morning by morning they gathered it, as much as each needed; but when the sun grew hot, it melted.

EXODUS 16:13-21

God has led the people out of slavery in Egypt and they are now beginning their long journey through the desert. The people complain and look back to the food they enjoyed in Egypt and want to return.

You may have heard of *Manna*. This passage describes God sending *Manna* for the people to eat—literally *Manna* means "What is it?", so it appears in verse 15 even though the translation doesn't include the word here.

An *omer* is an ancient unit of volume used for grain and other dry goods.

- Read the passage through once.
- Keep a few moments of silence.
- Read the passage a second time with different voices.
- Invite everyone to say aloud a word or phrase that strikes them.
- Read the passage a third time.
- Share together what this word or phrase might mean and what questions it raises.

Reflection   STEVEN CROFT

Bread of heaven

Bread plays a powerful part in the story of God's people. On the night God led the Israelites out from slavery in Egypt, the people were commanded to bake unleavened bread to take with them. At Passover all down the years, the Jewish people have remembered the Exodus by eating bread without yeast for seven days (Exodus 13:3-9).

In the journey through the wilderness, Israel learned to depend on God for daily bread: the manna which fell from heaven. There was just enough for that day, provided directly through God's grace.

In the countryside around Galilee, crowds followed Jesus out into the desert. Jesus took just a few loaves and gave thanks, broke the bread and gave it to the people. Jesus makes it clear that this gift of physical bread is a sign of his gift of the deeper spiritual food which we need. Jesus himself is the bread of life (John 6:35).

Through the wilderness, Israel learned to depend on God.

Again, in an upper room on the night before he died, Jesus celebrated a meal with his friends at Passover. He "took a loaf of bread, and when he had given thanks, he broke it and said: 'Take, eat. This is my body that is for you. Do this in remembrance of me' " (see 1 Corinthians 11:24).

All of these stories about bread should be in our minds when we pray this line of the Lord's Prayer. It is this line, with its double stress on "this day" and "daily," that has led many Christians to use the Lord's Prayer every day as the heart of their own personal prayers.

Praying for ourselves?

At first sight, "Give us this day..." looks like a prayer for ourselves. The Lord's Prayer began with a focus on God (praise) then moved on to prayer for others (known as intercession) and now we come to prayer for ourselves (petition).That's a good order for our own prayers.

But look more closely. "Give us this day..." is indeed a prayer for ourselves but it's a very modest prayer, and it is this modesty which is life-changing.

In Janis Joplin's most famous song, "Mercedes Benz," she asks the Lord for not only the luxury car of the title, but also a color TV and a night on the town. Perhaps when we first approach prayer we think it's about asking for the good things of life for ourselves.

Greed shapes so much of our culture and there is a distortion of Christianity which is based on coming to Jesus and growing rich in material goods (it's called the prosperity gospel). But the Lord's Prayer is the opposite. It is the antidote to greed and wanting more and more.

For Jesus teaches us to ask (and therefore to want) just enough. Not wealth. Not a big house. Not new clothes. Just bread. And just enough bread for today. "Give us this day..." is a prayer that teaches us to be content with enough (and that means it is indeed, in its way, a passport to great happiness).

> **In short**
>
> In the Lord's Prayer Jesus teaches us the importance of asking God for what we need. At the same time it reminds us only to ask for "just enough"—not everything we might want, simply what we need.

For discussion

- How easy or difficult do you find it to pray for your own needs? Is there a particular way you shape your prayers?
- How would your attitude to money and possessions be reshaped by praying this prayer and meaning it every day? How would the world be reshaped if everyone prayed like this?

Physical and spiritual food

Daily bread is a gift from my Father in heaven. It is a sign of God's provision and love. If I can see my relationship with God in something as basic and ordinary as bread then surely I can see the other things in my life as provided by God and be deeply thankful for them: my home, my possessions, my family, my friends, my work.

As I pray this prayer, my perspective changes. My Christian faith is not only about part of my life. My Christian faith is about the whole of my life.

For every meal, I need to give thanks. For every moment, I give thanks. At the end of the day, I give thanks. I live my life in a relationship with the maker of the world.

The prayer overcomes the gap between the physical and the spiritual. For some people in history there has been a separation of the spiritual and the physical. We compartmentalize our lives. But, with this idea of bread, the Lord's Prayer helps us connect the whole of our lives, physical and spiritual.

We are certainly praying for something physical: real bread for our real bodies. But we are also praying for something spiritual—Jesus the living bread, the food for our souls. Longing for Jesus himself is near the heart of the prayer. We are not *just* physical bodies but we *are* physical bodies.

Father, give us all we need for our whole selves to thrive. Give us living bread each day. Give us Jesus.

> **In short**
> Praying for daily bread encourages us to give thanks for everything in our lives, from the most basic upwards. It also reminds us that we have spiritual as well as physical needs.

For discussion

- How can you build into your day reminders and moments of thanksgiving to God for all his many gifts?

- What difference does it make that the prayer says "Give us this day…" rather than "Give me this day…"?

Concluding Prayer

Almighty God, Father of all mercies, we your unworthy servants give you most humble and hearty thanks for all your goodness and loving kindness. We bless you for our creation, preservation, and all the blessings of this life, but above all for your immeasurable love in the redemption of the world by our Lord Jesus Christ for the means of grace and for the hope of glory. And give us, we pray, such a sense of all your mercies that our hearts may be unfeignedly thankful and that we show forth your praise not only with our lips but in our lives by giving up ourselves to your service and by walking before you in holiness and righteousness all our days; through Jesus Christ our Lord, to whom, with you and the Holy Spirit, be all honor and glory, now and for ever. **Amen**.

THE GENERAL THANKSGIVING
(ADAPTED FROM THE BOOK OF COMMON PRAYER)

Sending Out

Reflect this week on your own approach to money and possessions. How can you see them more as gifts from God? How far does a desire for more shape your life?

Reflect as well on the challenge of saying a prayer of thanks, a grace, before each meal. Is this something you could learn to do?

These readings may help you in your reflections:

Wants are the bands and cements between God and us.

THOMAS TRAHERNE (C. 1636–74)

People hold cheap what they see every day of their lives, but when confronted by extraordinary events are dumbfounded, though these events are truly no more wonderful than others. Governing the universe is a greater miracle than feeding five thousand people with loaves of bread, but no one marvels at it. People marvel at the feeding of the five thousand not because this miracle is greater, but because it is out of the ordinary. Who is even now providing nourishment for the whole world if not the God who creates a field of wheat from a few seeds?

AUGUSTINE (354–430)

We do not complain of what God does not give us; rather we thank God for what he does give us daily.

DIETRICH BONHOEFFER (1906–45)

FORGIVE US OUR SINS AS WE FORGIVE THOSE WHO SIN AGAINST US

pilgrim

The aim of this session is to explore the central place of forgiveness in the Christian life: both receiving God's forgiveness and extending forgiveness to others.

Opening Prayers

O God, make speed to save us.
O Lᴏʀᴅ, make haste to help us.

Wash me through and through from my wickedness
and cleanse me from my sin.

PSALM 51:2

Oh, how good and pleasant it is,
when brethren live together in unity!

It is like fine oil upon the head
that runs down upon the beard,

Upon the beard of Aaron,
and runs down upon the collar of his robe.

It is like the dew of Hermon
that falls upon the hills of Zion.

For the Lᴏʀᴅ has ordained the blessing:
life for evermore.

PSALM 133

Then Peter came and said to him, "Lord, if another member of the church sins against me, how often should I forgive? As many as seven times?" Jesus said to him, "Not seven times, but, I tell you, seventy-seven times."

MATTHEW 18:21-22

Heavenly Father,
forgive the sins which tear us apart;
give us the courage to overcome our fears
and to seek that unity which is your gift and will
through Jesus Christ our Lord.
Amen.

BASED ON EPHESIANS 3:16-19

Share with the group a memory of leaving home.

Reflecting on Scripture

Reading

Then Jesus said, "There was a man who had two sons. [12]The younger of them said to his father, 'Father, give me the share of the property that will belong to me.' So he divided his property between them. [13]A few days later the younger son gathered all he had and travelled to a distant country, and there he squandered his property in dissolute living. [14]When he had spent everything, a severe famine took place throughout that country, and he began to be in need. [15]So he went and hired himself out to one of the citizens of that country, who sent him to his fields to feed the pigs. [16]He would gladly have filled himself with the pods that the pigs were eating; and no one gave him anything. [17]But when he came to himself he said, 'How many of my father's hired hands have bread enough and to spare, but here I am dying of hunger! [18]I will get up and go to my father, and I will say to him, "Father, I have sinned against heaven and before you; [19]I am no longer worthy to be called your son; treat me like one of your hired hands." ' [20]So he set off and went to his father. But while he was still far off, his father saw him and was filled with compassion; he ran and put his arms around him and kissed him. [21]Then the son said to him, 'Father, I have sinned against heaven and before you; I am no longer worthy to be called your son.' [22]But the father said to his slaves, 'Quickly, bring out a robe—the best one—and put it on him; put a ring on his finger and sandals on his feet. [23]And get the fatted calf and kill it, and let us eat and celebrate; [24]for this son of mine was dead and is alive again; he was lost and is found!' And they began to celebrate.

[25]"Now his elder son was in the field; and when he came and approached the house, he heard music and dancing. [26]He called

one of the slaves and asked what was going on. ²⁷He replied, 'Your brother has come, and your father has killed the fatted calf, because he has got him back safe and sound.' ²⁸Then he became angry and refused to go in. His father came out and began to plead with him. ²⁹But he answered his father, 'Listen! For all these years I have been working like a slave for you, and I have never disobeyed your command; yet you have never given me even a young goat so that I might celebrate with my friends. ³⁰But when this son of yours came back, who has devoured your property with prostitutes, you killed the fatted calf for him!' ³¹Then the father said to him, 'Son, you are always with me, and all that is mine is yours. ³²But we had to celebrate and rejoice, because this brother of yours was dead and has come to life; he was lost and has been found.'"

LUKE 15:11-31

Explanatory note

Within Judaism, feeding pigs—which were considered to be profoundly unclean—would probably have been the most demeaning occupation possible.

Fathers in Ancient Near Eastern culture maintained their dignity at all costs, it would almost have been unheard of for a Father to run in public; that he does so here shows the depth of his love for his son.

● Read the passage through once.

● Keep a few moments' silence.

● Read the passage a second time with different voices.

● Invite everyone to say aloud a word or phrase that strikes them.

● Read the passage a third time.

● Share together what this word or phrase might mean and what questions it raises.

Reflection

STEVEN CROFT

Receiving forgiveness

There are two elements to this part of the prayer, and the second builds on the first. The first is a simple prayer for forgiveness—one that we are called to make as often as we say the prayer. The second connects the forgiveness we can receive from God to the forgiveness we extend to others.

What are we asking forgiveness for? This is the line of the Lord's Prayer where the traditional and the contemporary language versions on p. 12 are most different.

What are we asking forgiveness for?

The traditional version has the word "trespasses": "Forgive us our trespasses as we forgive those who trespass against us."

A trespasser is someone who crosses a line to walk where they should not walk. The word in English carries something of the meaning of the words in the original but not everything. It communicates that what we are asking forgiveness for is our wrong actions: the times we really have done things wrong. But the Bible makes clear that we need to go deeper. We often need to seek God's forgiveness for our thoughts and words as well (see Matthew 5:21-30).

So is "sins" any better? It's not a word in common use any more except in religious contexts. It translates the word found in Luke's version of the prayer which carries the meaning of missing the mark or falling short in our behavior. It's a deeper and more comprehensive term than trespass.

Some English translations attempt a more literal translation of the term used twice in Matthew's version of the prayer and once in Luke: "Forgive us our debts." The same meaning is caught brilliantly in the parable of the two sons, which follows Jesus' saying about forgiving another person seventy-seven times (Matthew 18:23-35). "Debts" carry the idea that something is lacking and something is owing in our relationship with God or our relationship with others. The parable also helps us get into proportion our own debt to God with the debts others owe to us.

> *"Sins" carries the meaning of missing the mark or falling short in our behavior.*

Whatever term you prefer, the deeper notion here is that our sins can be forgiven. We should not think of God forgiving us as an easy matter (any more than it's easy for us to forgive other people). For God to open up the way of forgiveness to us meant sending his Son to die on the cross for our sins.

The Lord's Prayer at this point would be meaningless without the Lord who gives us the prayer and who gave his own life so that we can be reconciled to God. The parable of the two lost sons and their father would be meaningless without the Son who told it, and whose sacrifice makes reconciliation possible.

The parable of the two sons makes clear the need for two kinds of reconciliation in our relationship with God. The younger brother represents the journey of the person who comes back to God after years of rebellion, wandering away and going his own way. The elder brother represents us all as we continue in the Christian life. There are moments in all of our journeys where we realize that, even though we are part of the family, we need to seek the Father's forgiveness.

In short

The simple power of the fourth phrase of the Lord's Prayer is the knowledge that we can be forgiven for what we have thought, said, and done. We all need forgiveness and reconciliation both with God and with each other, and in the Lord's Prayer we pray for this forgiveness each time we say it.

For discussion

- Is your own faith story more like the younger brother in the story or the elder brother?

- Which word in the prayer is most helpful to you: trespasses, sins, or debts?

- Do you find it easy or more difficult to accept that you are forgiven?

Forgiving others

A wise person once said that the parts of the Bible he found most difficult are not the parts that are hard to understand but the parts that are as clear as day.

The second half of this line of the Lord's Prayer could not be easier to understand. We are called to forgive others when they sin (or trespass) against us. Our willingness to forgive others is related to God's forgiveness of us. God's grace to us and our obligation to others go hand in hand.

God longs for us to live not in isolation but in community.

There is a mercy here though it can seem a severe one. God in his mercy longs for us to live not in isolation but in community with others. That community is expressed in friendships, in families, in marriage for those called to be married, in the family of God's people, the Church, and in our wider society.

Any community is a community of imperfect people. Therefore any community we are part of will be spoiled by unkind words, hurtful actions, slander and gossip, or wrong attitudes.

Without forgiveness there can be no lasting community.

For discussion

- The elder brother in the story finds it very difficult to welcome and receive the younger brother when he comes home. Is that in any way part of your experience in the life of the Church?

- How do you think that there can be more forgiveness in families, among friends, and in the Christian community?

Concluding Prayers

As our Savior taught us, so we pray: **Our Father**... (see p. 12)

Most merciful God,
we confess that we have sinned against you
in thought, word, and deed,
by what we have done,
and by what we have left undone.
We have not loved you with our whole heart;
we have not loved our neighbors as ourselves.
We are truly sorry and we humbly repent.
For the sake of your Son Jesus Christ,
have mercy on us and forgive us;
that we may delight in your will,
and walk in your ways,
to the glory of your Name.
Amen.

Sending Out

During this coming week reflect on this line of the Lord's Prayer and what it means.

You may want to reflect especially on whether it would be helpful to make a special prayer of confession to God either in private or with a priest as you prepare for baptism and confirmation.

You may also want to reflect on whether there are particular people or situations in your life where God is calling you to extend forgiveness to others.

These readings may help you in your reflections:

> Forgive me, O Lord; O Lord, forgive my sins, the sins of my youth, and my present sins, the sin that my parents thrust upon me, original sin, and the sins that I cast upon my children, in an ill example; actual sins, sins which are manifest to all the world, and sins which I have so labored to hide from the world, and that now they are hid from mine own conscience, and mine own memory. Forgive me my crying sins, and my whispering sins, the sins of uncharitable hate, and sins of unchaste love, sins against thee and thee, against thy power, O Almighty Father, against thy wisdom, O glorious Son, against thy goodness, O blessed Spirit of God.
>
> **JOHN DONNE (1571-1631)**

> Sorrow for sin is necessary, but it should not involve endless self-preoccupation. You should dwell also on the glad remembrance of the loving kindness of God.
>
> **BERNARD OF CLAIRVAUX (1090-1153)**

> Our courteous Lord does not want his servants to despair even if they fall frequently and grievously. Our falling does not stop his loving us.
>
> **JULIAN OF NORWICH (1373-1417)**

LEAD US NOT INTO TEMPTATION
BUT DELIVER US FROM EVIL

pilgrim

The aim of this session is to explore this plea to God for help and protection.

Opening Prayers

O God, make speed to save us.
O Lord, make haste to help us.

The Lord is my light and my salvation;
whom then shall I fear?

The Lord is the strength of my life;
of whom then shall I be afraid?

Though an army should encamp against me,
yet my heart shall not be afraid;

And though war should rise up against me,
yet will I put my trust in him.

One thing have I asked of the Lord; one thing I seek:
that I may dwell in the house of the Lord all the days of my life;

To behold the fair beauty of the Lord
and to seek him in his temple.

God is faithful, and will not let you be tested beyond your strength, but with the testing he will also provide the way out so that you may be able to endure it.

I bind unto myself today
the strong name of the Trinity,
by invocation of the same,
the Three in One, and One in Three.
Of whom all nature hath creation;
Eternal Father, Spirit, Word:
Praise to the Lord of my salvation,
salvation is of Christ the Lord.
Amen.

FROM ST. PATRICK'S BREASTPLATE (HYMNAL 1982, 370)

Conversation

Has your journey in the Christian faith so far been easy or difficult? What kind of difficulties have you experienced?

Reflecting on Scripture

Reading

Therefore take up the whole armor of God, so that you may be able to withstand on that evil day, and having done everything, to stand firm. [14]Stand therefore, and fasten the belt of truth around your waist, and put on the breastplate of righteousness. [15]As shoes for your feet put on whatever will make you ready to proclaim the gospel of peace. [16]With all of these, take the shield of faith, with which you will be able to quench all the flaming arrows of the evil one. [17]Take the helmet of salvation, and the sword of the Spirit, which is the word of God.

[18]Pray in the Spirit at all times in every prayer and supplication. To that end, keep alert and always persevere in supplication for all the saints.

EPHESIANS 6:13-18

Explanatory note

The image that Paul uses here is the image of the armor used by the soldiers of the Roman army. If you want to picture what he is talking about you might like to find an image of a Roman legionary.

- Read the passage through once.
- Keep a few moments' silence.
- Read the passage a second time with different voices.
- Invite everyone to say aloud a word or phrase that strikes them.
- Read the passage a third time.
- Share together what this word or phrase might mean and what questions it raises.

Reflection ROBERT ATWELL

The reality of evil

What are we asking God for in this last petition of the Lord's Prayer? The prayer to do God's will, to have sufficient food to eat, to forgive and be forgiven appear straightforward, though, as we have seen, their meaning is profound. What is the human reality behind a plea for help in the face of temptation and evil?

In all sorts of ways we see evidence of progress in the world: the eradication of some diseases, the decrease of child poverty, better housing for the vast majority of citizens, and a quality of life our grandparents would never have dreamed possible. For all this we give thanks, but it is not the whole story.

Not everyone in the world shares equitably in the benefits progress generates. There are vast inequalities of wealth, and life expectancy varies greatly not only between nations, but even between areas of the same country.

The Old Testament prophets rail against a world where dog eats dog. They condemn injustice of every kind. Amos, for example, rebukes corrupt corn traders who manipulate scales to defraud poor people and make easy money (Amos 8:4-6).

We rejoice in human progress, but the Bible forces us to look deeper and sees a more complicated picture, a world in which "all have sinned and fall short of the glory of God" (Romans 3:23).

All of us are vulnerable to temptation, to being "economical with the truth," or sacrificing our principles when it suits us. When bad things happen it is tempting to scapegoat, to pick on individuals or groups of people who can be blamed for our ills. It is easy to nurse resentment or allow jealousy to poison our relationships. Which may be why Jesus tells us to pray constantly for God's help and guidance. He recognizes the weakness behind our bravado.

Jesus' words are not easy to translate. In some versions they are rendered, "Lead us not into temptation"; in others, "Save us from the time of trial"; and in yet others, "Save us from being tested." None of us likes being tested in case we are found wanting. It may be this idea lies behind Jesus' words.

Peter in his First Letter talks about faith being tested by the difficulties life throws up, much in the way that gold is tested in the assayer's fire for its purity (1 Peter 1:7). However Jesus' words are translated, they recognize our fundamental vulnerability and our need of God.

Mercifully, as Paul reminds us, "God is faithful, and he will not let you be tested beyond your strength, but with the testing will also provide the way out so that you may be able to endure it" (1 Corinthians 10:13).

That said, Paul never glosses over the reality of evil in the world. Nor should we. The twentieth century may have seen extraordinary scientific, economic, and intellectual progress, but it also witnessed a larger number of people killed in conflict than in any other epoch. Thanks to the combined efforts of Adolf Hitler, Joseph Stalin, and Mao Tse Tung, it is estimated that 188 million people were killed. We rightly pray, "Lord, deliver us from evil."

In short

Despite the progress of the world in which we live, we will all be tempted from time to time and we have certainly all seen quite how terrible the consequences of evil are. This should give fervor to our prayer.

Paul recognized a level of conflict within himself. "I do not understand my own actions. For I do not do what I want, but I do the very thing I hate" (Romans 7:15). Where do you experience conflict in your life?

Sometimes a whole generation can be held captive by an idea or a philosophy that is a lie and denies our humanity. Hitler persuaded the German people that the Jews were the cause of their economic and social problems in the 1930s. Where is the battleground today?

The armor of God

This is the background to the language of spiritual warfare which we find in the New Testament and throughout Christian spiritual writing. Paul alerts us to the battle of ideas that goes on in every generation. The values and priorities of a society shape its life, and that ideological struggle is as real today as it was for the people who lived in Ephesus to whom he was writing 2,000 years ago.

We may be vulnerable to temptation, but we are equally vulnerable to being manipulated or undermined, which is why we need God's protection. It is why Paul encourages the Ephesians not to be complacent, but actively to clothe themselves with God's own armor.

The values of truth, justice, peace, and integrity.

The sort of fighting that Paul describes does not use guns or suicide bombers. God wants us to use different weapons, the sort that lead by example, that cajole and beckon, that persuade and inspire others to a better way of life. God's weapons are the belt of truth, the breastplate of justice, the shoes that risk the journey to forge peace, the great shield of faith, the helmet of salvation, and the sword of the Spirit. Christians are to be people of integrity, as well as passion.

> **In short**
> One way in which we can avoid temptation is through protecting ourselves by wearing God's own armor, which includes consciously adopting the values of truth, justice, peace, and integrity.

For discussion

- The Celtic monks like Patrick (see the opening prayers on p. 48) developed a form of praying using Paul's language about the armor of God. They were called "breastplate prayers." As the monks dressed each day they would consciously pray that God would clothe them with his heavenly armor. How might you bind to yourself God's protection?

Concluding Prayers

As our Savior taught us, so we pray: **Our Father**... (see p. 12)

Eternal light, shine into our hearts,
eternal goodness, deliver us from evil,
eternal power, be our support,
eternal wisdom, scatter the darkness of our ignorance,
eternal pity, have mercy upon us;
that with all our heart and mind and soul and strength
we may seek your face and be brought by your infinite mercy
   to your holy presence;
through Jesus Christ our Lord.
Amen.

ALCUIN OF YORK (804)

Sending Out

During this coming week reflect on this line of the Lord's Prayer and what it means.

You may want to reflect on your strengths and weaknesses: giving thanks to God for your strengths and praying that you never become complacent or arrogant; and on your weaknesses praying that God will strengthen and protect you.

These readings may help you in your reflections:

> When we pray "And lead us not into temptation" we should know that the Lord is teaching us inwardly. The words reassure us that the adversary can do nothing against us because all is ultimately within the control of God. The words put us in touch with our vulnerability and inner weakness. But as we confess our need of God humbly and quietly, and surrender to God the glory that is properly his, then the prayer that is offered in the fear of God and to his honor will be met by his loving kindness.
>
> CYPRIAN OF CARTHAGE (C. 200-58)

> No wise person will deny the existence of evil in the world. I believe evil to be a perversion of mind and spirit, swerving away from the way of true virtue, which frequently overtakes us when we are unwary. The greatest danger does not lie outside us. It comes from our very selves: the enemy is within. Within us is the "father of lies." Within us, I say, dwells our adversary. Hence, we must examine our aims, explore our patterns of thought, and generally be vigilant over our thoughts and the desires of our heart.
>
> AMBROSE (C. 334-97)

> God, seeing the world falling into ruin through fear, never stops working to bring it back into being through love, inviting it back by grace, holding it firm by charity, and embracing it with affection.
>
> PETER CHRYSOLOGUS (C. 400-50)

> A Christian is an oak flourishing in winter.
>
> THOMAS TRAHERNE (C. 1636-74)

FOR THE KINGDOM, THE POWER, AND THE GLORY ARE YOURS NOW AND FOR EVER. AMEN

pilgrim

The aim of this session is to explore praise and worship as the place to begin and end our prayers and the end point of our lives.

Opening Prayers

O God, make speed to save us.
O Lord, make haste to help us.

Bless the Lord, O my soul,
and all that is within me, bless his holy name.

Lift up your heads, O gates;
lift them high, O everlasting doors;
and the King of glory shall come in.

"Who is the King of glory?"
"The Lord, strong and mighty,
the Lord, mighty in battle."

Lift up your heads, O gates;
lift them high, O everlasting doors;
and the King of glory shall come in.

"Who is he, this King of glory?"
"The Lord of hosts, he is the King of glory."

"Now my soul is troubled. And what should I say—'Father, save me from this hour'? No, it is for this reason that I have come to this hour. Father, glorify your name." Then a voice came from heaven: "I have glorified it and I will glorify it again."

Bring us O Lord God at our last awakening
into the house and gate of heaven,
to enter that house and dwell in that house
where there shall be no darkness nor dazzling but one equal light;
no noise nor silence but one equal music;
no fears nor hopes but one equal possession;
no ends or beginnings but one equal eternity;

in the habitations of your glory and dominion,
world without end.
Amen.

ERIC MILNER-WHITE (1963) AFTER JOHN DONNE (1631)

Let us bless the Lord.
Thanks be to God.

Conversation

**Which line of the Lord's Prayer do you find the most powerful—
and why?**

Reflecting on Scripture

Reading

The passage for this week is one of the great prayers of the Old
Testament, set in the context of the end of David's life when all has
been prepared for the building of the temple.

Then David blessed the LORD in the presence of all the assembly;
David said: "Blessed are you, O LORD, the God of our ancestor
Israel, for ever and ever. [11]Yours, O LORD, are the greatness, the
power, the glory, the victory, and the majesty; for all that is in the
heavens and on the earth is yours; yours is the kingdom, O LORD,
and you are exalted as head above all. [12]Riches and honor come
from you, and you rule over all. In your hand are power and
might; and it is in your hand to make great and to give strength
to all. [13]And now, our God, we give thanks to you and praise your
glorious name.
    [14]"But who am I, and what is my people, that we should be able
to make this freewill-offering? For all things come from you, and
of your own have we given you."

1 CHRONICLES 29:10-14

- Read the passage through once.
- Keep a few moments' silence.
- Read the passage a second time with different voices.
- Invite everyone to say aloud a word or phrase that strikes them.
- Read the passage a third time.
- Share together what this word or phrase might mean and what questions it raises.

Reflection   STEVEN CROFT

Praise and adoration

The final lines of the Lord's Prayer were not part of the prayer as Jesus taught it in the gospels. They were added at an early stage by the Church as the Lord's Prayer became widely used in public worship. The words draw on the text from Chronicles we have explored in this session.

The final lines of the prayer bring us back to the beginning. The Lord's Prayer begins in praise and adoration: "Our Father in heaven, hallowed be your name." We end where we began in worship and appreciation of God now and for all eternity.

The Christian view of humankind is that men and women were created to know God and live in a right relationship with God of love and fellowship. The Westminster Catechism begins with this question (in the older, non-inclusive language version):

What is the chief end of man?
The chief end of man is to know God and enjoy him for ever.

The word end here means not only our destiny—the end of the story—
but our purpose: all which gives our life a meaning.

The true point, perspective, and purpose in our lives is found in the
praise and appreciation of God and in our relationship with God. This
relationship, as we have seen, is at the heart of the Lord's Prayer.
Because of God's grace in Jesus Christ we are able to call God "Father";
we are drawn into a relationship with our brothers and sisters in
Christ. We align ourselves with God's will for a better world. We begin
to see that everything we have comes from God. We place ourselves
daily within his love, care, and protection.

> **In short**
>
> The full purpose of our lives is to praise God. As we do so we begin
> to recognize more and more that everything comes from God and
> to feel even more thankful and full of praise.

For discussion

- What is your own favorite way of praising God? On your own or
  with others? In church or in the open air? In your own words or
  in songs and hymns?

- Share a time when you have felt particularly full of praise for
  God. What caused it? How did you express it?

Worship

Why is the habit of praise and worship so vital? It is not, after all,
something that comes easily to most of us. Yet Jesus is clear that the
first commandment is to love the Lord your God with all your heart,
soul, mind, and strength.

The worship and praise of God gives us scale and orientation and direction for the whole of the rest of our lives. Worship is worth-ship—seeing God's worth and value in relation to the creation. As we see God's immense and surpassing value so everything else falls into perspective.

Worship is the center of what the Bible means by heaven.

We see the idols that the world worships for what they are: empty. Appreciating God's goodness and greatness is like appreciating a fine painting or a range of mountains. You can never come to an end of what it means.

The worship and praise of God opens our hearts to all that is good. The opposite of praise is criticism. Most of us can think of people who are by nature very critical of others: they have only to open their mouths and a stream of negative judgments comes out.

Criticism of others and of the world seems to close us down as people and narrow our horizons. Praise and appreciation opens out our words and then our hearts and minds—and especially the praise and worship of God.

Finally, to be caught up in praise and worship is to be caught up in the activity of heaven. The chief end of men and women will be to enjoy God for ever. Worship is the center of what the Bible means by heaven. Our worship on earth is connected to the praise and worship of heaven. Our worship on earth prepares us for eternity.

For every Christian, offering praise to God is a daily calling. We are called to worship not only with our lips but in our lives. That calling is sustained as we say our prayers, and especially the Lord's Prayer. However, our daily worship also needs to be sustained by gathering with God's people in praise and worship on Sundays and on other days of the week.

The Church gathers primarily for worship, to celebrate all that God is and all that God has done, to be drawn into the life of the Trinity: the Father, Son, and Holy Spirit. We offer God songs and words of praise in psalms, hymns, and spiritual songs. We attend to God's words in Scripture. We gather around the table of the Lord in the Holy Communion. We intercede for the needs of the world.

The final lines of the Lord's Prayer connect our own individual prayers—thin and weak as they often are—with the great hymn of praise of the Church in both earth and heaven, in time and in eternity:

For the kingdom, the power, and the glory are yours now and for ever. Amen.

In short

Worship helps to recognize who God really is, it opens our hearts to what is good and catches us up into the life of heaven. It is something we are called to every day of our lives and is fulfilled, among other ways, when we say the Lord's Prayer.

For discussion

- How do you find praise and worship rebalances your perspective?
- Is the worship of God in heaven something you look forward to?
- Looking back over these six weeks, what have you learned about the Lord's Prayer as a pattern for your prayers? What do you still need to learn about prayer?

Concluding Prayers

As our Savior taught us, so we pray: **Our Father**... (see p. 12)

The glorious company of apostles praise you.
The noble fellowship of prophets praise you.
The white-robed army of martyrs praise you.
Throughout the world the holy Church acclaims you:
Father, of majesty unbounded,
your true and only Son, worthy of all praise,
the Holy Spirit, advocate and guide.

FROM TE DEUM LAUDAMUS

Sending Out

During this coming week reflect on your overall pattern of worship and prayer and how you will aim to grow in prayer from this point on.

These readings may help you in your reflections:

> When has a time existed when God has not reigned? The kingdom of God is rooted in us through the blood of Christ's passion, and we have the privilege of being its first subjects. We pray, therefore, that we may reign with Christ, sharing in his sovereignty, as he has promised.
>
> CYPRIAN OF CARTHAGE (C. 200–58)

> Think of a musician tuning a lyre. By skill the musician adjusts the high notes to the low, and the intermediate notes to the rest, and so produces a series of harmonies. So too the wisdom of God holds the world like a lyre and joins things in the air to those on earth, and things in heaven to those in the air, and brings each part into harmony with the whole. By his decree and will he regulates them

all to produce the beauty and harmony of a single, well-ordered universe.

ATHANASIUS (295–373)

Almighty God who has supreme power over everything, being himself supremely good, would never permit the existence of anything evil among his works if he were not so omnipotent and good that he can bring good even out of evil. Thus, what is that which we label evil other than an absence of good?

AUGUSTINE (354–430)

What does union with God mean? It is not a nice feeling we get in devout moments. That may or may not be a bi-product of union—probably not. It can never be its substance. Union with God means every bit of our human nature transfigured in Christ, woven up into his creative life and activity, absorbed into his redeeming purpose, heart, soul, mind, and strength. Each time it happens it means that one of God's creatures has achieved its destiny.

EVELYN UNDERHILL (1875–1941)

NOTES

Session One
Augustine (354–430), *Confessions*, X.
Cyprian of Carthage (*c.* 200–58), *On the Lord's Prayer*, 9.
Irenaeus (*c.* 130–*c.* 200), *Against Heresies*, III, 20, 2.
Te Deum Laudamus, *Common Worship: Daily Prayer*, London, Church House Publishing, 2004, p. 636.

Session Two
Cyprian of Carthage (*c.* 200–258), *On the Lord's Prayer*, 14.
Jean-Pierre de Caussade (1675–1751), *Abandonment to Divine Providence*, II, 3.
John Dominic Crossan and Jonathan L. Reed, *Excavating Jesus: Beneath the Stones, Behind the Texts*, London, SPCK, 2002, pp. 274–5.
The Iona Community Worship Book, Glasgow, Wild Goose Publications, 1991.
C. S. Lewis, *Mere Christianity*, The Christian Library edition, Uhrichsville, OH, Barbour Publishing, 1995, p. 74.
Brian McLaren, *The Story We Find Ourselves In*, San Francisco, Jossey-Bass, 2008, p. 132.
The Rich, The Poor and the Future of the Earth, Christian Aid Report, London, Christian Aid, April 2012.

Session Three
Augustine (354–430), *Commentary on St John's Gospel*, 8, 1.
Dietrich Bonhoeffer (1906–45), *Life Together*, ET John W. Doberstein, SCM Press, 1954, p. 16.
Thomas Traherne, (*c.* 1636–74), *Centuries of Meditations*, 1.

Session Four
Bernard of Clairvaux (1090–1153).
John Donne (1571–1631), *Sermon*, 107.
Julian of Norwich (1373–1417), *Revelations of Divine Love*, 39.

Session Five
Ambrose (*c.* 334–97), *On the Six Days of Creation*, 1, 31.
Peter Chrysologus (*c.* 400–50) Sermon, 147.
Cyprian of Carthage (*c.* 200–58), *On the Lord's Prayer*, 25.
Thomas Traherne (*c.* 1636–74) *Centuries of Meditations*, IV.

Session Six
Athanasius (295–373) *Against the Pagans*, 42.
Augustine (354–430) *Enchiridion*, 11.
Cyprian of Carthage (*c.* 200–58) *On the Lord's Prayer*, 9.
Eric Milner-White (1963) after John Donne (1631)
Te Deum Laudamus, *Common Worship: Daily Prayer*, London, Church House Publishing, 2004.
Evelyn Underhill (1875–1941), *The Light of Christ*, London, Longmans, Green and Co., 1944.